Sports Superstars

Joel Embiid

By India James

Torque

Bellwether Media · Minneapolis, MN

Torque™

Torque brims with excitement perfect for thrill-seekers of all kinds. Discover daring survival skills, explore uncharted worlds, and marvel at mighty engines and extreme sports. In *Torque* books, anything can happen. Are you ready?

This edition first published in 2025 by Bellwether Media, Inc.

Library of Congress Cataloging-in-Publication Data

LC record for Joel Embiid available at: https://lccn.loc.gov/2024047014

Editor: Kieran Downs Designer: Gabriel Hilger

Printed in the United States of America, North Mankato, MN.

TABLE OF CONTENTS

SHOOTS AND SCORES

The 76ers are playing the Spurs. Joel Embiid is on fire. His teammate passes him the ball. He dribbles it down the court. He dodges other players. He shoots. He scores!

Embiid just became one of the only players in the history of the **National Basketball Association** (NBA) to score 70 points in one game.

TOYOTA
21
76

WHO IS JOEL EMBIID?

Joel Embiid is a **professional** basketball player. He plays **center** for the Philadelphia 76ers. He is known for his scoring. He is also known for his ballhandling and **defense**.

Embiid is the first player born outside of the United States to lead the NBA in scoring. He was named the NBA **Most Valuable Player** (MVP) in 2023.

JOEL EMBIID

BIRTHDAY	March 16, 1994
HOMETOWN	Yaoundé, Cameroon
POSITION	center
HEIGHT	7 feet
DRAFTED	Philadelphia 76ers in the 1st round (3rd overall) of 2014 NBA Draft

BASKETBALL BEGINNINGS

Embiid was born in Yaoundé, Cameroon. He grew up in Cameroon with his parents, brother, and sister. He played volleyball and soccer when he was young.

ANOTHER SPORT

EMBIID THOUGHT ABOUT BECOMING A PROFESSIONAL VOLLEYBALL PLAYER WHEN HE WAS A KID.

YAOUNDÉ, CAMEROON

EMBIID WITH HIS MOTHER AND SON

Embiid started playing basketball when he was 15 years old. The next year, he came to the U.S. to play high school basketball.

Embiid played one year of college basketball at the University of Kansas. He was named the Big 12 Defensive Player of the Year. He had only been playing basketball for four years!

Embiid hurt his back at the end of the season. He had to miss some big games. But he still decided to enter the NBA **draft**.

FAVORITES

SPORT OTHER THAN BASKETBALL

soccer

SOCCER TEAM

Real Madrid CF

DRINK

Shirley Temple

TV SHOW

The Vampire Diaries

WATCHING THE GAME

EMBIID DID NOT KNOW MUCH ABOUT BASKETBALL AS A TEENAGER. HE LEARNED BY WATCHING VIDEOS OF NBA STARS.

TIME TO GO PRO

2014 NBA DRAFT

Embiid entered the NBA draft in 2014. Many people thought he would be the first pick. But he hurt his foot before the draft. The Philadelphia 76ers chose him as the third pick in the draft.

Embiid did not play in the 2014–2015 season. He hurt his foot again the next year. He did not play that season, either.

JOEL EMBIID MAP

Philadelphia 76ers
Philadelphia, Pennsylvania

2014 to present

Embiid had his **rookie** season in 2016–2017. He scored so many points that he was named to the NBA **All-Rookie First Team**.

Throughout the 2017–2018 season, Embiid's scoring helped the 76ers to their first winning season in five years. They made the **playoffs**. Embiid was named an NBA **All-Star** for the first time in 2018.

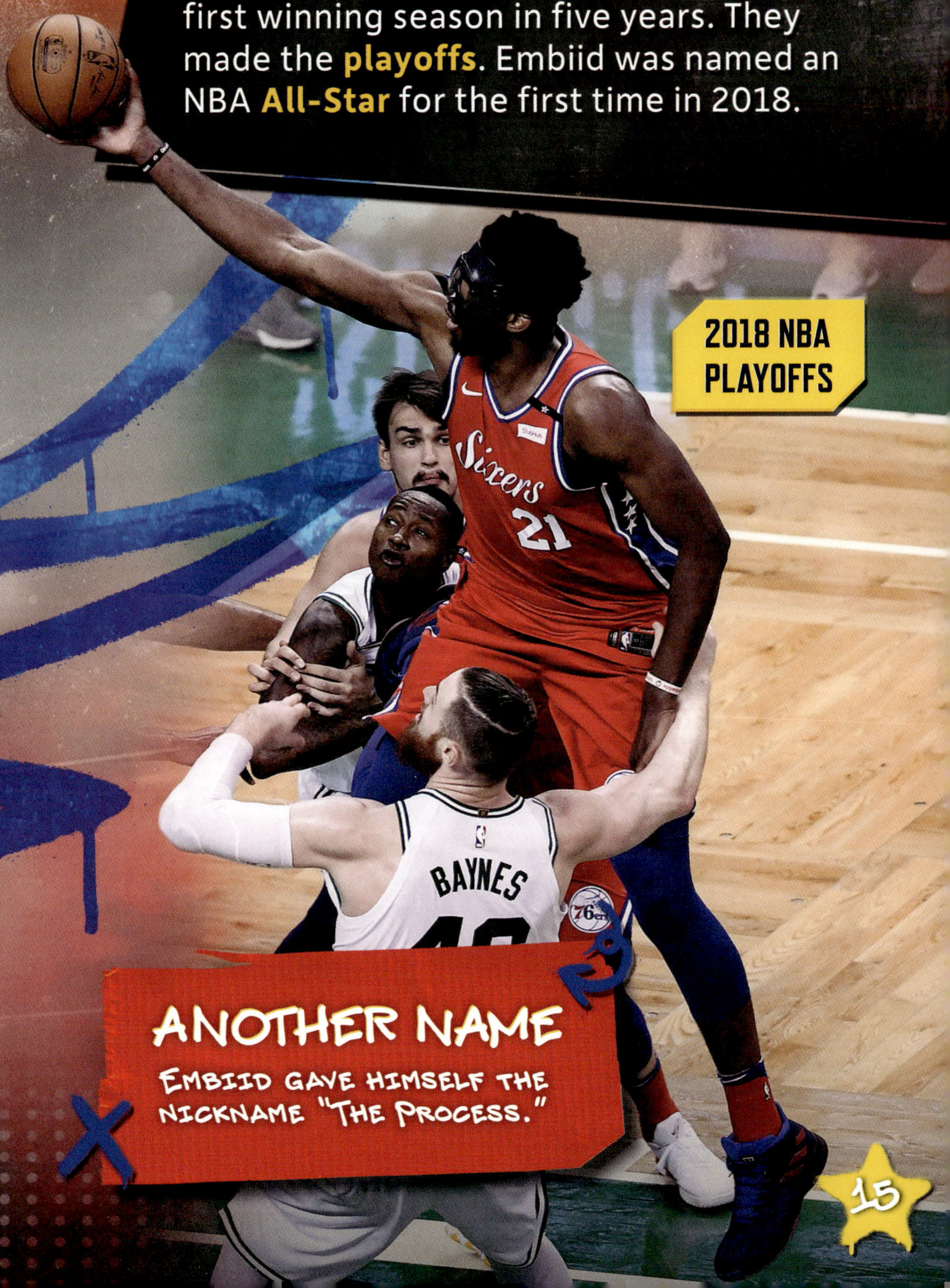

2018 NBA PLAYOFFS

ANOTHER NAME

EMBIID GAVE HIMSELF THE NICKNAME "THE PROCESS."

The 2018–2019 season was big for Embiid. He averaged 27.5 points and 13.6 **rebounds** per game. He was named an All-Star again.

Embiid became the first person born outside of the U.S. to win the NBA scoring title in the 2021–2022 season. He averaged 30.6 points per game!

MANY LANGUAGES

EMBIID SPEAKS ENGLISH, FRENCH, AND BASAA.

TROPHY SHELF

- NBA MVP
- Big 12 Defensive Player of the Year
- 7-time NBA All-Star
- Olympic gold medal
- 2-time NBA scoring leader

Embiid won the scoring title again during the 2022–2023 season. He was named the NBA MVP. He scored 70 points in one game during the 2023–2024 season. He was the ninth player in NBA history to do so.

Embiid played for Team USA at the Paris **Summer Olympics** in 2024. He helped the team win gold!

THREE COUNTRIES

EMBIID IS A CITIZEN OF CAMEROON, THE U.S., AND FRANCE.

TIMELINE

— 2014 —

Embiid is drafted by the 76ers

— 2022 —

Embiid wins the NBA scoring title

2024 PARIS SUMMER OLYMPICS

— April 2023 —

Embiid wins the NBA scoring title for the second time

— May 2023 —

Embiid is named the NBA MVP

— 2024 —

Embiid helps Team USA win a gold medal at the Paris Olympics

EMBIID'S FUTURE

Embiid loves Philadelphia. He has set up a **charity** to help people in his city. His charity is named for his brother, Arthur, who passed away in 2014.

Embiid signed a 3-year deal with the 76ers in 2024. He has overcome many challenges. Embiid hopes to help his team keep winning!

GLOSSARY

All-Rookie First Team—an honor in the NBA for the best rookies in a year

All-Star—a player named as one of the best players in a league

center—a player in basketball who often blocks shots and gets rebounds

charity—an organization that helps people in need

defense—a group of players who try to stop the opposing team from scoring

draft—a process during which professional teams choose high school and college players to play for them

most valuable player—the best player in a year, game, or series; the most valuable player is often called the MVP.

National Basketball Association—a professional basketball league in the United States; the National Basketball Association is often called the NBA.

playoffs—games played after the regular season is over; playoff games determine which teams play in the championship game.

professional—related to a player or team that makes money playing a sport

rebounds—when players take control of basketballs after missed shots

rookie—a first-year player in a sports league

Summer Olympics—a worldwide summer sports contest held in a different country every four years

TO LEARN MORE

AT THE LIBRARY

Fishman, Jon M. *Joel Embiid.* Minneapolis, Minn.: Lerner Publications, 2020.

Hewson, Anthony K. *Joel Embiid.* Minnetonka, Minn.: Kaleidoscope Publishing, 2019.

Kim, Cheryl. *Joel Embiid: Basketball Star Shooter.* North Mankato, Minn.: Capstone Press, 2023.

ON THE WEB

FACTSURFER

Factsurfer.com gives you a safe, fun way to find more information.

1. Go to www.factsurfer.com
2. Enter "Joel Embiid" into the search box and click 🔍.
3. Select your book cover to see a list of related content.

INDEX

The images in this book are reproduced through the courtesy of: Chris Szagola/ ASSOCIATED PRESS/ AP Images, front cover; PA Images/ Alamy, p. 3; Tim Nwachukwu/ Staff, pp. 4, 4-5, 19 (2023), 20; Elsa/ Staff/ Getty Images, p. 6; Mitchell Leff/ Contributor/ Getty Images, pp. 7, 14, 21; Sid MBOGNI, p. 8; Matt Slocum/ ASSOCIATED PRESS/ AP Images, p. 9; Icon Sports Wire/ Contributor, p. 10; Kansas City Star/ Contributor/ Getty Images, pp. 11, 15; grey_and, p. 11 (soccer); evren mörel/ Alamy Stock Vector/ Alamy, p. 11 (Real Madrid CF); raptorcaptor/ Adobe Stock, p. 11 (Shirley Temple); Justin Stephens/©CW Network/courtesy Everett Collection/ Everett Collection, p. 11 (*The Vampire Diaries*); Kathy Willens/ ASSOCIATED PRESS/ AP Images, p. 12; Michael Perez/ ASSOCIATED PRESS/ AP Images, p. 13; Brian E Kushner, p. 13 (map); Vaugn Ridley/ Contributor/ Getty Images, p. 16; Dustin Satloff/ Stringer/ Getty Images, p. 17; DeFodi Images/ Contributor/ Getty Images, p. 18 (medal); DAMIEN MEYER/ Contributor/ Getty Images, pp. 18-19; Ronald Cortes/ Contributor/ Getty Images, p. 18 (2022); Xinhua/ Alamy, p. 23.